The Chief

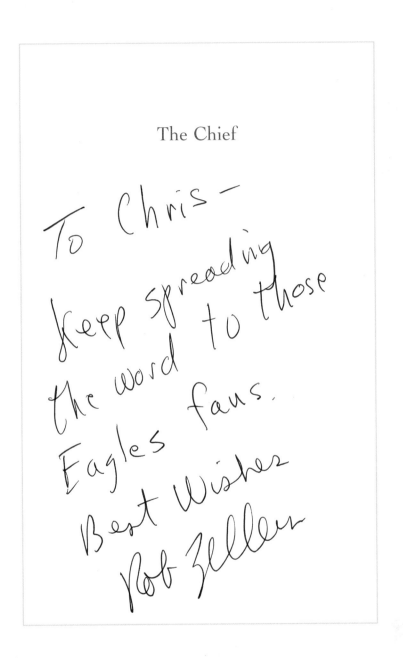

To Chris —
keep spreading
the word to those
Eagles fans.
Best Wishes
Rob Zeller

Tom Atkins as Arthur J. Rooney in *The Chief,*
Pittsburgh Public Theater.
Courtesy of Suellen Fitzsimmons.

The CHIEF

Rob Zellers
and
Gene Collier

✦

With a Foreword by
Art Rooney Jr.

University of Pittsburgh Press

Published by the University of Pittsburgh Press,
Pittsburgh, Pa., 15260
Copyright © 2008, Rob Zellers and Gene Collier
All rights reserved
Manufactured in the United States of America
Printed on acid-free paper

10 9 8 7 6 5 4 3 2 1

Library of Congress Cataloging-in-Publication Data

Zellers, Rob.
  The chief / Rob Zellers and Gene Collier ; with a foreword
by Art Rooney, Jr.
      p. cm.
  ISBN-13: 978-0-8229-4358-7 (cloth : alk. paper)
  ISBN-10: 0-8229-4358-1 (cloth : alk. paper)
  1. Rooney, Art, 1901-1988—Drama. 2. Pittsburgh Steelers
(Football team)—Drama. 3. Football—Drama. I. Collier,
Gene. II. Title.
  PS3626.E365C48 2008
  812'.6—dc22
                                              2008015839

Treat everybody the way you'd
like to be treated. Give them the benefit
of the doubt. But never let anyone mistake
kindness for weakness.

Arthur J. Rooney

Contents

Foreword

Art Rooney Jr.

Hello, I'm Art Rooney Jr., and my father was the Chief. Two of my younger brothers, Pat and John, gave the Chief his moniker, as he would say. ("Moniker" is ArtRooneyspeak. In meeting a stranger, he would sometimes ask, "What's your moniker?"—and then, very often, be obliged to restate the question.)

Pat and John, who are twins, were faithful watchers of a 1950s-vintage television show in which Superman, played by George Reeves, masqueraded as an unassuming newspaper reporter named Clark Kent. One of the principal characters in the show was a gruff but lovable editor called "the Chief." Pat and John, perceiving similarities of style and personality between Clark Kent's boss and the owner of the Steelers, began referring to our dad by that name.

Others picked up on it—first the people who worked in the football team's offices on the ground floor of the Roosevelt Hotel, then the players, coaches, and sportswriters. By the 1970s, when the Steelers were winning Super Bowl championships, Art Rooney was the Chief to almost everyone.

But only behind his back. To address him that way was unthinkable. All five of his sons called him "Dad." Friends who belonged to the same generation called him "Art." If you were not in either category, he could only be "Mr. Rooney." In fact, "Mr. Rooney" was the title of a television documentary tracing his career as a horseplayer (maybe the best there ever was), sports entrepreneur, and venerated Pittsburgh folk hero.

Once, in his presence, a recently hired Steeler secretary uttered the forbidden moniker. Instantly, she found herself the focus of every eye in the room. Looks of astonished disapproval made her see her mistake. The Chief himself, pretending not to have noticed, let it pass.

He was aware—couldn't help but be—that the public, along with his colleagues, friends, and ac-

quaintances, in due time thought and spoke of
him as the Chief. Whether or not he took pleas-
ure in this, no one could tell. Art Rooney Sr. was
a genuinely humble man who loved adulation.
The most casual observer could tell that he was
humble, but only those who were close to him
saw the interesting paradox in his nature.

He had a grandfather who worked in a steel
mill and a grandfather who worked in a coal
mine. His father owned a saloon on the North
Side. He was a gifted athlete in his youth, and
even more gifted at living by his wits. "Don't be a
sap," he would say. And, "Think ahead of the
play." His advice to his sons was: "Treat people as
you would like to be treated, but don't let anyone
mistake kindness for weakness."

He was charismatic and smart. He was gener-
ous to those in need. He made friends quickly
and easily. Rich men and poor men, the high and
mighty and the down and out, solid citizens and
hustlers, bishops and bums were happy to be in
Art Rooney's company. However he may have
felt about it, the Chief was a name that suited
him.

Starting in the 1980s, I kept a handwritten journal in which I jotted down stories about my father and the Damon Runyon characters in his circle of friends. When Gene Collier of the *Pittsburgh Post-Gazette* asked if he could use these sketches of mine for a play he was writing with Rob Zellers, I immediately told him to go ahead. Collier is an excellent sports columnist with keen senses of humor and irony. He was just the guy who could recreate Art Rooney, it seemed to me. Some years before, Collier had intended to write a book about my father—a project he ultimately gave up—and that was when he first saw my scribbling. I did not know Rob Zellers but discovered him to be an accomplished all-around dramatist who had worked with August Wilson, among others, at Pittsburgh Public Theater.

The one-man play that Zellers and Collier decided to call *The Chief,* which has had five successful runs at Pittsburgh Public Theater in Pittsburgh, was every bit the achievement I had hoped it would be. In fact, it keeps getting better every year. In the title role, Tom Atkins has somehow incorporated my father's voice inflections,

speech patterns, mannerisms, and relaxed amia-
bility into his own style of acting. His ninety-
five-minute monologue is a riveting performance,
uncannily true to life.

I know that what the audience sees is Art
Rooney and his world as it really existed, and I
know because I was there.

Introduction

Gene Collier

The most successful single play in the long and distinguished profile of Pittsburgh Public Theater began among the far-flung little wildfires of oral history. Art Rooney Jr., the second of the Chief's five sons, was chewing the fat with two of his writer buddies, Baltimore newspaper legend John Steadman and later Mort Sharnik of *Sports Illustrated*. Both urged him to commit the rich American stories of his father to a journal, if not as aspiring literature, than as a precious gift to posterity. That was 30 to 40 years ago, or something like a decade before Art Jr. actually got around to it.

Though stories of the Chief, by the Chief, and for the essential understanding of the Chief had long been part of the oral tradition of western Pennsylvania, and often far beyond, the most critical conversation didn't happen until the new century. It was in the winter of 2001, on the campus of Carnegie Mellon University, and we dare say it was between us, the would-be coauthors, who had no clue they would be coauthors when the conversation started.

Had one of us not been the director of education for Pittsburgh Public Theater, and had the other's son not been preparing for the theater's annual Shakespeare contest, and had the former not arranged for some coaching sessions on that particular wintry Saturday in Oakland, this conversation would be part of no one's oral history and the play would likely never have happened. But in just a few short minutes, it was somehow revealed that Rob Zellers, who was in possession of a tribute titled "If The Chief Asks, We're Not So Good Today" that he'd been holding since 1989 written by a young columnist from the *Pittsburgh Press* named Gene Collier, had a long-held idea for a one-man play, and that Gene Collier had a long-held ambition to write a biography, and that their subjects were the very same Arthur J. Rooney.

In our separate cases, "long-held" meant, literally, "I'll never get this done, but I'm thinking about it." But at the introduction of potentially complementary "skill" sets—those of a long-time sportswriter who knew the Chief and the Steelers and a veteran theatrical presence who regarded Rooney's very aura as a kind of dramatic phenomenon, opportunity seemed to be pounding on the door with a shovel. Or was it a football helmet?

"Maybe I'd like to collaborate with you on that," said the sportswriter, who immediately heard that voice in his head reply, "What the hell are you saying?"

Neither of us had time to write a play, a problem verily dwarfed by the other problem: neither of us knew how to write a play. That second part would eventually be confirmed by some pretty impressive people. Tom Atkins, the great American stage actor whose stentorian voice we actually had the nerve to imagine would speak these lines some day, read through our first draft and said, "This will never work." Ted Pappas, the decorated director and producing artistic director of

Pittsburgh Public Theater, validated those in-
stincts by burying the script in a towering stack
of other unread scripts. Subsequently, an all-star
cast of extra-theatricals, including Dan Rooney,
the Steelers' chairman and the Chief's eldest son,
Jim Rooney, the Chief's politically astute grand-
son, the aforementioned Art Jr., and Roy
McHugh, the brilliant former columnist and
sports editor of the *Pittsburgh Press*, all found the
original script by various degrees underwhelming.

At that point, we could almost hear the some-
times-scathing monotone of Hall of Fame coach
Chuck Noll, who might have said of this theatrical project, as he once did about a troubled running back, the play had many problems, and they
were great.

One was wrapped up in the unorthodox nature of the collaboration. With full-time jobs and
families, the writers rarely wrote from the same
room. The play was not so much written as con-
jured from a seemingly endless, manic game of e-
mail ping-pong. Rob would serve a scene or an
anecdote to Gene, Gene would swat it back, or
fail to do so. Gene would slice some monologue

swatch to Rob, Rob would serve it back, a promising volley would ensue, until someone swatted the thing into the crab dip. Then we'd throw the whole scene out with the crab dip. Once, we lined up page-by-page the typed versions of months of literary spasms on tables in the theater's rehearsal hall so we could literally walk through the play reading it aloud to each other. We ran out of rehearsal hall.

Another of the play's great problems was the Chief himself, whose story is little less than the sprawling epic of an American century. Arthur J. Rooney was a gem, by general agreement, but displaying all of the bright and dark facets to their full polish in anything approaching the correct proportions is a rather monstrous undertaking.

Every once in a while, Gene would ask the exceedingly reasonable question, "Tell me again why we're doing this?" Since Rob did not have anything resembling a reasonable answer, we just kept going. When it was more or less completely rewritten the tenth time, Ted Pappas gave it a read. Even more notably, he came back with some suggestions that did not include a wastebasket and a match. Apparently, the collected stories, characters, and events were compelling — in fact, so compelling that Ted thought some of it must have been fictitious. These things couldn't have actually happened. The Immaculate Reception? C'mon.

At approximately the same time, Roy McHugh got back to us with some notes on the original script, some bright red marks that led us straight to another level of authenticity. "The Chief," McHugh wrote, "would never say this." Or this. Or this. He might say this. Soon after that, Art Jr. mentioned that the newest script had the feel of the exact cadence of his father, the right phrasing, the right places for elaboration and reflection.

By now, the play was developing its own oral history. Myron Cope and Ed Kiely contributed stories and observations, as did Dan Rooney. Jim Rooney met with us for the third or fourth or fifth time at a North Side sandwich place, and explained that we still didn't quite have it, particularly as the script attempted to reveal how the Chief would explain the relationship among his greatest teams, the city, and the fan base. Atkins was doing his own research, turning up at Steeler headquarters on draft day, 2003, huddling with Ed Bouchette, the authoritative Steelers beat writer for the *Pittsburgh Post-Gazette*, about what the Chief's habits were around the office. Atkins interviewed North Siders and acquaintances, and searched his own memory of having met the Chief when he was a young boy.

Among the rapid-fire aspects of this project that were finally becoming clear was that the people closest to the Chief wanted what wound up on the stage to be correct, and they did not want it whitewashed. As the Patriarch himself had said, "I touched every base."

Though the project had clearly established its own inertia, and to some extent its own little buzz, the coauthors were only slightly closer to real validation than when they started. Then one day, Pappas decided that this was a worthy project and that the theater would present *The Chief*. That meant the serious rewriting could begin toward an actual production on the stage of one of America's great theaters. It was like being informed that you are officially an astronaut, and

INTRODUCTION

xxi

that the countdown has begun. *The Chief* would follow *The Mikado* in fall 2003. Gilbert and Sullivan followed by Zellers and Collier.

In a series of intense sessions during the summer of 2003, the play was workshopped in a conference room overlooking Penn Avenue, where its 19th nervous rewrite was fueled primarily by the line-by-line analysis of the people who would bring it to dramatic life: Pappas, Atkins, and dramaturg Kyle Brenton. A team of exquisite designers were engaged for set, costumes, lighting, and sound, and we were on our way.

The Chief debuted that November and has now been on The Public's stage for five emotionally charged runs. Sometimes men cry at it, which is often a surprise to women who might have wandered in indifferently but get caught up in where all the laughter is going. It is perhaps the one Pittsburgh arts entity on which the reliable theater crowd joins Joe from Munhall in his Bradshaw jersey for the same joyful purpose. To say the coauthors have been gratified beyond imagination by Pittsburgh's response to *The Chief* would only begin to explain things.

The families and descendants of many of the characters Atkins reminisces about on stage are often seen in the lobby afterward. Some 30 members of Billy Conn's family have seen the play. Franco Harris brought groups. Jim Leyland could be heard laughing uproariously from the balcony. Rocky Bleier and many of the Steelers from the '70s have been spotted, and Andy Russell, who handed the Chief the game ball after the club's first Super Bowl championship, joined Dan Rooney on stage to present Atkins with a ball on the night of the show's premiere. A woman e-mailed us to say that the best time she'd had in years was going on a "date" with her husband that included some tailgating in a lot across the street from the theater. The children of Art Rooney II, the club's president, told their dad that being at *The Chief* was like getting to know their great-grandfather. Two guys drove in from California. Not California, Pa., the other California. Ernie Accorsi, then the general manager of the New York Giants, flew in expressly to see *The Chief*. The late Myron Cope, seated ringside, was surprised to hear Atkins divert from the script (as he did often and to great effect) to give him a big, "Oh, hi Myron!"

Ultimately, there is no escaping the conclusion that while the play works for many, many reasons, it works mostly due to one person, Art Rooney. All of the complex social and cultural elements that defined Pittsburgh in the first part of the 20th century produced a singular metropolitan character, and that city's greatest most enduring character was Art Rooney. That still undersells him in a way, as no combination of time and place can fully explain his humor, his way, or his humanity. In a place that sometimes has a hard time feeling good about itself, we like to think that maybe the Chief came back to remind us that not only was that OK, but that it was right.

Production Credits

The Chief received its world premiere at
Pittsburgh Public Theater, November 2003.

Directed by Ted Pappas
Set and costume design by Anne Mundell
Lighting design by Phil Monat
Sound design by Zach Moore
Dramaturgy by Kyle Brenton
Production stage manager — Fred Noel
Assistant stage manager — Alison Paleos

Cast — Tom Atkins as Arthur J. Rooney

Director Ted Pappas with Tom Atkins.
Courtesy of Suellen Fitzsimmons.

The Chief

The set of *The Chief*, complete with Arthur J. Rooney's original desk, designed by Anne Mundell and dressed by Gay Kahkonen, Kelly Yann, Todd Kulik, and Justin Pelissero.

Courtesy of Suellen Fitzsimmons.

rthur J. Rooney's office, March 1976. Desk piled high with stuff. On the shelves and wall are dozens of trophies, memorabilia, awards, plaques, and photographs (many askew), a chalkboard, humidor, a film/video screen, etc.

An audio montage of Steeler broadcasts and other sounds and music of Pittsburgh life is heard.

At curtain's rise, AJR is sitting in a desk chair reading a newspaper. He is dressed in a sport jacket, sweater, and shirt, and maybe the pants to a tuxedo. The tux jacket, shirt, and bow tie are on a hanger on the coatrack near the door.

At the conclusion of the montage, AJR drops the paper, notices the audience, reaches for the phone, and dials.

AJR:

Listen, will you call the Knights for me? Ask for Ice Pick. Huh? Just ask for Ice Pick Kelly. They'll put him on. Tell Ice Pick we'll be there at 7:45. Yeah. I thought we'd show up right before dinner. Yes, I got the tuxedo. I'm wearing it.

THE CHIEF

(Looks at the audience as he realizes they can see he is not wearing the tux.)

Yes, it fits. You're going to have to help me with the tie. And would ya tell Kelly to open that back door. We'll go right across the alley. *(Listens.)* No, no, no. I am not paradin' 'round the block in a tuxedo. What would people think?

(Pauses to listen; emptying his pockets onto the desk, pulling out a thick wad of money wrapped in a gum band, his rosary beads, a pocket watch, etc.)

That's right . . . right. And Kass, can you bring my speech? Yes, "that old crumpled thing." I have it? Why would I have it? I don't have it. It's in the drawer in the front hall. Yah, it's there.

Okay, thanks. Be there in a while. Yes. I'm going to say hi to a few folks here. Okay, bye.

(Hangs up.)

Hwaar ya?

Big affair at the Knights of Columbus tonight. They're making me one of the Elevated Knights, which I guess means I'm fit to defend the Pope. If the Pope needs me to defend him we're all in trouble, although I recall on occasion having to knock somebody's block off on his behalf. Howard Cosell is the master of ceremonies. Lots of people would like me to knock his block off. NFL Films is going to be there. They're doing a story about me. The model football organization and all that. You *know* they're going to make me out to be some big shot. I'm not a big shot. I'm just a dems and dose guy. That's the truth. Maybe I'll just sit here and let the whole evening slip my mind. Old guys forget, ya know?

But then I'd miss a free dinner. What would Mc-Cormick say about that! Use to loaf with Chris McCormick from when we were kids. He was a big accountant in town. And I do mean BIG! Biggest, fattest guy on the North Side. Loved to go to the pictures. Used to go to the Kenyon Theater up on Federal Street, but eventually he couldn't fit in the seats any more. He got the owner to build him a special seat. Twice the regular size, his backside was that big. Never was anyone could eat like McCormick . . . 'less it was one of his sisters. Two sisters big as him. Me and my brother Dan used to go over there for Sunday dinner sometimes when we were kids. My God how that family could eat! Pitchers of gravy, biscuits, whole hams, desserts. It went on for hours! I think they only stopped cuz they got tired.

One time McCormick came on the train with us to New York. Going to a fight up there at Yankee Stadium. It was Carnera versus Ernie Schaaf. I'll never forget it. Schaaf went down in the 13th. Never woke up. Died a few days later in the hospital. When the fight was over, we went back to Manhattan to get the train home. Everybody was hungry and the train's not there, it's runnin' late, so we go into a steak house across the street from Penn Station. Jimmy Shine's. Nice place. There's 10, 12 of us, maybe. We all ordered a steak and then somebody went across the street to check on the train. Just as the waiters are putting our food on the table, the guy comes back from Penn Station and yells, "Let's go, the train for Pittsburgh is leaving in five minutes." So I grab my kick and throw down some cash, and everybody else bolts out of the place. Except McCormick. He just sits there. The look on his face! I thought he was gonna cry. He was looking from one steak to another to another. I said, "Chris, we gotta go," and I start for the door. I see out of the corner of my eye, McCormick grabs a tablecloth from the next table and starts dumping the steaks one by one into the tablecloth. I get into the station and I see the rest of our guys wavin' to me to hurry up. But I'm laughin' too hard to hurry too much. I stop and turn to see if McCormick is gonna make the train. And, oh my God. Here he comes. What a sight! 400 pounds, jigglin' and jogglin' all over the platform. Big sack of meat over his shoulder like Santa Claus. I thought he was going to die right there. He was breathin' like a racehorse. Breathed like that all the way to the Horseshoe Curve in Altoona. But he got his steak. No train was gonna take his steak.

Chris McCormick and I were friends for 50 years. He did eventually eat himself to death. One steak too many. God bless him.

THE CHIEF

(He goes to the coat rack and grabs the tux.)

Whaddya think?

Howard Cosell. NFL Films. James Michener is gonna be there. He wants to write a book about me. Pretty big stuff. I hate the whole business! They all get a kick out of talking about me, but they don't know. I'm just a kid from the Ward, a horseplayer, a bootlegger. I just got lucky—stuck with it—and finally got the ring. But you can't say that in a speech at the Knights of Columbus, can ya?

(Searches pocket for matches and finds the speech.)

The speech. Well, I guess it isn't in the drawer in the front hall after all.

(Begins to read.)

Ladies and Gentlemen, fellow Knights, when we played the Vikings in that first Super Bowl. . . . Forget it. I'll save that for Howard Cosell. Let me show you something.

(Searches for and finds the picture of him receiving the trophy.)

In the locker room, after that Vikings game. I didn't know what was going on. It was pandemonium. There were TV lights everywhere. One moment I was congratulating our players, handing out tobies, the next, all of a sudden, I was on national TV and Pete Rozelle was presenting me with the Super Bowl trophy. There was a day when I could not have imagined anything *like* a Super Bowl, let alone winning it. I ran the club for 40 years without a championship. Eight winning seasons in all those years! I was just lucky to keep it going. By the late '60s we had become the joke of the National Football League. It was my boys, Danny and Artie, and Chuck Noll. They're the ones who brought the Super Bowl trophy to Pittsburgh. Everyone knows that. They're the ones that deserved the attention. And they were nowhere to be seen.

(Points again at the picture he is holding.)

See? Here it is. That's the trophy. That's Rozelle. I helped him get the job of commissioner. I look like I don't know where I am here. I remember all of a sudden everything got quiet. I looked around the room and everything had stopped. Someone said later that there was not a dry eye in the house. For being such tough-guys, that team was sure actin' like a bunch of softies. That look on my face? I was just thinkin' about where we were gonna go for dinner. I'd forgotten to eat anything all day.

I'll see all my old friends at the Knights of Columbus tonight. Some of them go all the way back to the First Ward. They knew me when. They'll be the ones that stay down in the bar, even during dinner. Part of me will want to stay down there too. Break out the pretzels and start a poker game. Kass would prefer I not do that. Then the accolades will begin. They'll exaggerate it. They'll have me saving the city of Pittsburgh. They'll have me healing the sick and the lame. I'll get another plaque for the wall. You ever see so many plaques for an old North Sider? I grew up

NFL Commissioner Pete Rozelle presenting the Super Bowl
trophy to Arthur J. Rooney after Super Bowl IX, 1975.
Courtesy of the Pittsburgh Steelers.

right here on the North Side—on General Robin-
son Street. The First Ward. What a collection!
Lotta good families. Hard working people. But a
lotta characters too! Mostly Irish. Came over
here during the potato famine. A few Polish and a
few blacks who didn't mind being around us.
You'd hear Jimmy Dulin speakin' the Irish with

his pals in the tavern. Mrs. Pacharski yellin' at her kids in Polish. "Wracajcia do domu." I can still hear her. And Nate Goldstein. He was the only Jewish guy. He owned a clothing store. Donated a lot of things back to the community, but because he was a Jew, we still had to protect him. And we had our share of thugs and crooks in the Ward. Yes. Can you imagine that? In the First Ward? Well, life was tough. We were all poor. Some were really bad off. Us kids didn't think about it much. I was too busy playin' ball at the playgrounds. My dad owned a saloon across the street from Expo Park. That's where the Pirates played before they moved to Forbes Field . . . it was right on the spot where Three Rivers Stadium would eventually be built.

Isn't that ironic? We call it family history.

I used to go swimming in the river right where the Gateway Clipper Fleet ties up to let Steeler fans off to go to the game. Used to love to swim out behind the stern-wheelers and ride their wake back to shore. You ever swim in the Allegheny? You think it's dirty now! You should have seen it then! Sewage. Garbage. Waste from the factories and steel mills. Every once in a while you'd see a dead horse float by. On the level! Used to worry my mother sick that we would play down there so much. I even swam in the river one day when I had no intention of swimming in the river. It was before flood control, when the Allegheny would overflow every time somebody spit in it practically. It was nothin' for us to leave for school by going out a second-floor window. Get in a skift. You know, like a canoe. One day there were three of us paddlin' to school in this skift. Me and my brother Dan and Squawker Mullen, friend o' ours, paddlin' right through the outfield at old Exposition Park. Well, Squawker's movin' around so much in the skift that I have to yell at him, Squawker, you sit still. Does he sit still? No. Do we go swimmin' on a day when we don't want to go swimmin'? Yes.

Well, Dan and Squawker, they do okay. I see them make it to the wooden grandstand in left field and hang on. But me, I had boots and an overcoat on. Which is no way to swim. Do you

THE CHIEF

11

remember seeing that Mark Spitz climbin' out of the pool at the Olympics on TV? Didn't have boots and an overcoat on, did he? I was on my last gasp on God's earth when I got to that grandstand. I almost never saw Three Rivers Stadium because I almost drowned in it 60 years before!

That's more of that irony! It sort of follows the Irish around.

Actually, my father was born in Wales. His family had gone there to work. One time he went to get a life insurance policy and the broker, who was also Irish, started givin' him a rough time. "All these years you're telling everyone you're Irish, and you were born in Wales!" Pop never skipped a beat. "Hey, if a cat has kittens in the oven, you don't call 'em biscuits!"

(Pointing to a picture of Mayor David L. Lawrence.)

You know who this is? This is Davey Lawrence. He was my oldest and closest friend.

(Pointing again.)

Here's my good friend Billy Conn. I'll tell you a story about him in a minute.

(Takes the picture he was looking for off the wall.)

Here it is. This is Rooney's Cafe and Bar. Nickel beers and free lunches. Those were our living room windows. I think that was mine and my brother Dan's room there. All those banners, musta been election day. Everyone came to the saloon for political discussion. Well, all right, not everyone. Some just came to get loaded. An Irishman with a few pints in him is prone to talk politics, though. And a bunch of them together in a tavern usually meant a brawl or two as well. Being a fair-minded man, my father'd always give a warning before he knocked a noisy yegg off his barstool. My dad's shirts always started out the night clean and white, but they got to look like a butcher's apron from the fights. On a Saturday night, he would come clompin' upstairs three or four different times to change his torn and bloody shirt. But he always had us up and out of the house on Sunday morning for early Mass.

Rooney's Cafe and Bar. Courtesy of the Rooney family.

And if James Michener wants to write about me, then chapter one in that book would have to be about the Church. The Church is what kept us steady, bad times and good. Gave us hope when we didn't have much else. We went to Mass. That was the only thing you needed to know. You just went. That was it. Well, I guess if you wanted to, you could miss Mass. But you'd better be dead. And God knows there was enough of them to choose from: Sunday morning Mass. Mass every morning of the week. Saturday evening Mass. Midnight Mass on Christmas Eve. Easter. All Saints Day. Holy Days of obligation they called 'em. They'd throw 'em in all over the calendar just to keep you off balance. Ascension Thursday, Assumption Tuesday, Retention This, Reduction That. Feast of the Immaculate Reception . . .

(Looks around at the audience to see if they caught this.)

Just checkin' to see if you're paying attention.

Later, when I was on the road a lot and going to churches in New York and Chicago and Washington, I saw some very well-to-do congregations. It was another world from little St. Peters over here on the North Side. I don't think the folks in those fancy parishes ever had to defend their turf with their fists or run a poker game to feed a neighborhood. You'd be surprised the things poverty can make you do. Things that can ruin your future, let alone your clear conscience. How this all stacks up at Judgment Day, I don't know.

THE CHIEF

I'm not even sure I know how it stacks up at the Knights of Columbus tonight.

(The phone rings. It's Kass.)

Hullo. You can't find it? That's because I have it here. You were right. Yes. (*Listens.*) We don't have to be there until 8:15! That's great! Okay. Be home soon. Bye.

I have some more time now. Okay. Where were we?

Well if I told you about the Church, I have to tell you about boxing. Because if one didn't work, you always had the other. My brother Dan had more knockouts than Jack Dempsey. Some even came inside the ring. When there wasn't a ballgame going on at Expo Park, they'd sometimes set up for a circus or carnival. The carnival always had a washed-up boxer and you could win a buck for every round you could stay on your feet with him. Those guys couldn't fight. If they could fight, they wouldn't be in the carnival. Our only problem was that if we knocked him out in the first round, we'd only get a dollar. One day, Dan

climbed into the ring with this pug from the
Johnny J. Jones Carnival—or was that the fighter's name? I don't know. Anyway, Dan carried
this guy for three rounds. Then I got into the ring
next . . . and Jones had a little time to rest so he
came bobbin' and weavin' and snortin' his way at
me. I just got in my stance and held my ground.

*(Demonstrates how it was done. He's having a good
time now.)*

I barely touched the guy and his nose was bleed-
in' like someone had turned on the "spicket," one
eye was swollen shut, and he started to slump so
I got him over on the ropes, and we sort of grunt
and lock up with each other. He wanted to fall
down. I wouldn't let him. And this went on for
three more rounds. Then my younger brother
Jim got in the ring and held Mr. Jones up for another three rounds. It crossed my mind that we
were going to kill this guy for nine dollars. We
got our money, but when they came back the next
year the carnival manager showed up at my father's saloon and gave him five bucks to keep us
kids away from his fighter.

I've always been a fighter. Not just street fighting.
I was the AAU lightweight champ. I got chosen
for the Olympic boxing team in 1920, but I
couldn't go because I was playin' baseball for
money at the time. Wheeling Stogies.

Down through the years, I still got the chance to
put on the gloves myself. Our second head coach,
Luby DeMeolo this was, All-American in his
playing days. We weren't getting along too well.
Bunch of us were loafin' at the Sherwyn Hotel
one afternoon, arguing about boxers versus football players, who was tougher and all that, and
Luby says, "You know what, you think you're
such a tough guy. I'd like to take you on."

I didn't know what he meant. I said, "At what?"

"Boxing," he says. On the level.

I said, "Are you sure?" "Sure," he says. I got on
the phone to Joe Getz, guy that used to clean our
uniforms. He had a lot of sports equipment. I
said, "Bring those gloves you got down there."
He says, "Ya want the big ones for foolin' around
or the real ones."

THE CHIEF

Arthur J. Rooney boxing card, 1918.
Courtesy of Murray Cards.

"Bring the real ones," I says. So we pushed back all the furniture against the walls.

Well, I was gonna go easy on him, but he wouldn't stop his yappin' so I gave him a couple of good ones. There he was, laid out on the dining room floor. I felt bad about it—I really did—but not for too long. Come to think of it, I had to duke it out with Joe Bach too, on the train coming back from a loss in Boston. He was our third head coach. Three head coaches in our first three years in the league, and I had to knock two of 'em out. That was a management practice that I eventually had to discontinue.

Okay then. I promised you a story about Billy Conn. In the '30s and '40s, Pittsburgh was loaded with professional fighters. Fritzie Zivic. Kid Dugan. Harry Greb from Garfield—Billy's hero. Six guys around here held titles. Of course, Billy Conn was the best of them all.

Billy's brother Jackie was also a fighter. Billy calls me one time and asks can I give Jackie a job. I said c'mon Billy, you know Jackie won't show up for a job. So Billy says well look at it this way, would you want him around? Billy and Jackie and their other brother Frank, and their dad, Westinghouse. They would go out on a given night and clean out an entire bar. Then before the night was over they'd get into an argument, split up, and go two on two among themselves.

I had to break up a fight once between Billy and his father-in-law and nearly got killed doin' it. Billy had just got married. We were at a party at Jimmy Smith's house in Greenfield. That was Billy's father-in-law, Greenfield Jimmy Smith—a character in his own right. Jimmy played for the old New York Giants, the baseball Giants, and he had never wanted Billy to marry his daughter Mary Louise. Beautiful girl. Some of you probably know Mary Louise. The fight broke out in the kitchen. Jimmy made one crack too many. I still remember Billy comin' off that stove where he was sittin'! I got between the two of them and just about got shoved through a window. They banged away at each other a little. And Billy broke a knuckle on his left hand—it was bad enough that they had to postpone the rematch with Joe Louis. Pound for pound, Billy was the greatest fighter of all time. Light heavyweight champion of the world, and came within a couple minutes of becoming the heavyweight champ. Against Louis in 1941. Nobody gave Billy a chance. Pittsburgh was on the edge of our seats. The Pirates stopped play in the middle of the game that night and piped in the radio broadcast over the PA. Players sat in the dugout and listened along too. Delayed the game an hour. We thought he had it won. You all know the story. He outboxed the best heavyweight of all time for 12 rounds. Made Louis look bad, too. In the 12th, Billy says to Louis, "You're in a fight tonight, Joe." And Joe says, "I knows it; I knows it." All Billy had to do was stay away from him for one more round. But no, Billy told his corner men that he was gonna knock Louis out. And Joe was waitin' for him.

(Shaking his head.)

And Billy got knocked out instead.

THE CHIEF

Stubborn.

"What's the use in bein' Irish?" Billy said, "If ya can't be dumb?"

When I got out of boxing, I had my only brush with actual work. My cousin, Matt Concannon, got me a job in the steel mill. Duquesne Works. Sweeping cinders. My first day, I had almost three hours in and it already feels like two hours too many. I was just starting to wonder how people worked that hard, day after day, year after year, when Matt called me aside and said, "Artie, you're doing real good; in 20 years you'll be a foreman like me." I asked him what his job paid and he told me. He was making less in a year than I was in one summer playing semi-pro baseball. And that was the last day—I didn't even pick up my pay—that was the last day I ever punched a time clock. I didn't have it in me to work in the mill. What they call an honest day's work just wasn't for me. Guys from the neighborhood could outwork you six ways from Tuesday. Women, seven ways. Stella Guier, one of our more demure North Side ladies, used to say she'd

Billy Conn vs. Joe Louis, 1941.
Courtesy of the Conn family.

outwork, outdrink, outswear anybody who came
into the Modern Cafe over on Western Avenue.
The men didn't care for that too much. One afternoon Stella had a snootful, and she was yellin'
about how she was the only one could drive a
wagon without the horses down Galveston Avenue, the real steep one with those, whaddya call
'em, hobblestones, and up onto the Manchester

Bridge and over the Allegheny River. They had hobblestones on that street so the horses could dig their hooves in 'em to pull the wagons up. It was steep, almost straight up. The Junior College is there now.

So Stella's yellin' about how she's the only one has the guts to try this, nobody else could do it. So the fellas got so tired of hearin' this. Finally told her, yer on! And I can remember practically the whole Ward turned out to watch the spectacle, not that they thought Stella could do it. They were kinda hopin' she might get killed tryin'. It was like goin' over Niagara Falls in a barrel. But now here she comes down Galveston, standin' on the wagon. Grippin' that big wagon tongue in her hands. The steel-covered wheels making a terrible racket on those hobblestones, and I'll be doggone, there she goes, all the way down, right up onto the bridge and over the river. Hit a big bump at the bottom, almost threw her off, but she held on. *(Pause.)* Stella Guier. She went right back to the bar to collect on the bet. She had a voice like that new city councilwoman, Sophie Masloff. She threw

open the door and yelled in, "You're all yella."
Stella Guier. She continued to be very unpopular.

(Lights his cigar.)

I don't think she ever married.

(To a member of the audience.)

Will this bother you? Yes? I'll put it out.

(Puts it out.)

I always have to put them out for Elsie Hillman,
you know. She says, "If you're going to visit King
Arthur, wear a gas mask!"

(The phone rings, AJR picks up.)

Hullo? Yah, hwaar ya? Good. What's up?

(Refers to The Daily Racing Form.)

. . . Right. Buttermilk Sky. No, the fifth at Aque-
duct. . . . Whaddya think? Even money. . . . He'd
better not.

(Raising his voice in laughter.)

You tell Gump I said that don't sound right, okay.

THE CHIEF

Even money, that's a good one. He's movin' up in class ya know. Tell Gumpy I'll call him tomorrow. . . . Okay, good.

(Hangs up.)

Even money. Everybody's got somethin' that they're good at without there bein' much explanation for it. Some call it "a knack." Best knack for me, no doubt, horseplayin'. Don't know why that is. But I could pick a winner, I could pick two, three in a day. Two, three in a row sometimes. I still can. There's a lot more to it than knowin' the ponies. You've got to know the trainers and the grooms and the kids who work in the barns. They tell me a lot—which horse likes the track, which jockeys are hung over—that sort of thing. Sometimes I just get a feeling. I just know. And when I get on a roll—when I'm playing with their money, so to speak—well, then I can really go. You need to be good at your arithmetic. You need to understand you're gonna lose some. You need finesse. Put all of it together, and it's called gambling. They don't put a tuxedo on it and put it behind a podium at the Knights of Columbus.

Once I took my friend Tom Murray with me to Pimlico. Some of you might know Tom. Prominent banker in town. Anyway, I had a horse running. Galveston Avenue was the horse's name. Wonder where I came up with that name.

Tom loved to tell this story later. We took the train to Baltimore. Tom noticed two guys on the train he thought looked kinda shady. Tom was a very proper type guy. Most everyone looked shady to him. I'm sure I looked kinda shady to him. We get to our seats at the track, in the clubhouse, and Tom turns around and sees these same two guys from the train are just a couple of rows behind us. He's getting very nervous. This was not a typical day in a banker's life. Just then one of my trainers came up to the clubhouse and says to me in this sort of loud whisper, "Galveston ain't feelin' good. He can run, but he's not gonna be very strong." So with that, I get up and leave the clubhouse like I'm goin' down to check on the horse. While I'm gone, the two shady characters walk up to Tom. One says, "I thought I heard that trainer say the horse ain't feelin' good.

What's goin' on?" Tom was scared stiff, but he managed to muster up, "Who wants to know?" So this guys says, "Look, we're with Mr. Rooney too. He gave us $4,000 to bet on Galveston Avenue. When's he comin' back? What are we supposed to do?" So Tom musta got some confidence from somewhere and tells 'em, "If Arthur said bet it, then bet it." Tom had $100 he was going to put on Galveston. He followed his own advice. Galveston took off like a shot. Didn't look very sick in fact. He won going away. I got back up to the clubhouse and Tom tells me the whole story.

(Feigning a dignified accent.)

"That's just about the most exciting thing that's ever happened to me, Arthur," he says.

But, he was a bit confused about what the trainer said. I told him, Tom, if the trainer walked into the clubhouse and announced to the world that Galveston was fit as a fiddle, he'd a gone off at even money. As it was, there must have been a lot of eavesdropping going on because he paid over $30 on a $2 bet. Tom won more than $1500 on his $100. My two associates, Iggy Borkowski and Richie Easton, who are really as gentle as the day is long—they just looked shady and mean—won more than $60,000 for me that day.

That's horseplayin'.

For an Irishman from the First Ward, it was pretty important to find somethin' you were good at. There weren't that many options. We were invited to move into the filthiest part of the city and work the most dangerous and dirty jobs. When we left Ireland we gave up starvation and discrimination, and in return we got discrimination and starvation . . . and opportunity. We eventually got good at the American way of life. Then we started to write some of the story ourselves. Coming from the Ward, you knew politics from the day you were able to speak. Like my dad taught me, politics is who gets what. And what I didn't learn about politics from my dad, I learned from Senator Coyne. Now there was a politician. When I was 20—so that'd be around 1921—I started to work for Senator Jimmy Coyne. He came to Pittsburgh from Galway in 1900. One of

16 children. Became Ward chairman then state senator. Republican, if you can believe it. Pittsburgh was 90 percent Republican in those days. Hey, I'm an Irish Catholic, pro-union, pro-working man, pro-integration Republican. Not too many of those around anymore.

I guess "lackey" would be the best way to describe my first job for the senator. I ran errands and set up chairs for political rallies. Voted for those who were sick.

(Pause to let that one sink in, and then by way of explanation.)

We knew who the sick would have voted for. Had they been well. It was no big deal then. Just politics.

Working for Senator Coyne meant that I could do some good in the Ward. That Charley Alldrich could work even though his left arm got pulled off by a tube rolling machine. That Mr. and Mrs. Mulvaney would not have their store rent raised —but that was mostly because I wanted to go out with their daughter. But that still counts as love thy neighbor. A lot of people relied on me. Remember, there was no welfare at that time. You had to take care of your own—especially if no one else liked your own. It was the system, and some of us got very good at it. I got so good at it I became a top lieutenant in the Coyne machine. I think I was a particular favorite of Senator Coyne, but I never forgot that it was really all about business. I was sitting in the senator's office one day when his secretary tried to interrupt with a phone call. The senator dressed her down for disturbing a meeting with his "great, good friend Mr. Rooney"—until she told him it was Mr. Mellon on the line then he banged my knees so hard pushing the desk away to get to the telephone that I was black and blue for two weeks.

I love politics. The backroom maneuvering and strategy. Getting things done. I hate it that you can't pick up a phone in this town and get a guy a job anymore. I've always liked politicians. Davey Lawrence and I played baseball together and boxed, and when we were too old we played poker and went to the racetrack. I still love to go

to the track with Tip O'Neill. All these Demo-
crats! But I guess I had too much of the Ward in
me to be a politician. I used to think it wasn't that
bad of a thing to have a few brothels in town. It
kept the nice young girls safe from the guys who
couldn't control themselves. Those guys had a
place where they could go. Now of course, you
don't get very far politically when you come out
strong for whorehouses.

That was my time in politics. Oh, no, wait. I did
run for public office once. Register of wills. I didn't
want to run. I only did it for Senator Coyne. I
am credited with one of the most unconventional
political speeches ever made. I told the people
and the reporters that I wouldn't know what to
do if I won and that I didn't even know where
the office was located, but that I would hire
somebody who would know how to do the job.
Time magazine heard about the speech and ran
the story under the heading, "At Last an Honest
Politician." And by the way, I gave that speech at
a picnic in the wrong county.

I lost.

Lucky break for me. And the taxpayers.

All the sick and deceased voters in the world couldn't keep Senator Coyne in office when orders for steel went down. I was lucky that I was so good at getting on to the next thing, even if some of those things became discredited over the years. My best aptitudes. Horses. Fighting. Gambling. Large, smelly cigars. The rules change. It's just the way the world keeps moving. You have to move along with it.

My sons and grandsons think I'm . . . less than forthcoming about the old days. Well, they're right. I guess I always thought that it was okay for me, but I didn't want it for them. I hung around enough political back rooms and after-hours joints. I had enough adventures for several generations of Rooneys.

I sometimes wonder if it was wrong to have had so much fun with it.

That's why one of the greatest thrills of my life was that my son Dan became such a good busi-

nessman. He got it right. In spades. Our kids—
the kids of all the owners: and I mean Mara of
the Giants, Halas of the Bears, Bidwill, Joe
Carr—all our sons made the successful transition.
When Dan took over the team he was the same
age I was when I bought the franchise. It was his
business from then on, but I insisted he deal with
matters the way our family always did. I just
don't want all the lessons to slip away in today's
game. Dan doesn't do everything the way I
would. But it's different now. He can't. He has a
whole bunch of assistants and attorneys and ac-
countants. He has his meetings at the Hilton or
the William Penn—we always met in McManus's
back room over some pigs feet and hard-boiled
eggs. And there're always TV cameras around
nowadays!

Now I walk around like a grandfather who spoils
the grandkids. I pass out cigars to the players,
take 'em to the track, hand out bonuses. Dan
wishes I'd pass out more cigars and less bonuses.

You know who really loves a good cigar? Joe
Greene.

Whenever I'm traveling and see a good cigar, I always bring one home for Joe. He likes to come into my office, sit right there and light one up, and just sit and talk. I tell him stories about the early days of the National Football League. He has a great appreciation for where we've been and what it took to get here.

Yes, he's the same one they call Mean Joe. Mean Joe Greene. Big misconception. There are a lot of misconceptions surrounding what we do. Since we're talking, let's get this straight about how I got the team in the first place. I know a lot of you think I won it at the racetrack. I did not win the team at the racetrack.

Back in 1933, when the NFL was just starting up, Charlie Bidwill, who owned the Chicago Cardinals, approached me about a team in Pittsburgh. I had run some booze with him during Prohibition.

Well, Charlie knew I was a successful promoter. And he said he could get a team for me. They were starting up a team in Philadelphia, and

Arthur J. Rooney and Joe Greene, 1972.
Courtesy of the Pittsburgh Steelers.

Pittsburgh would make a natural rivalry. The
state was about to repeal the blue laws that would
not allow football on a Sunday. I actually called
in some favors to help it along a bit. The entrance
fee was $2,500. They'd have given it to me for
nothin' if I'd put up a fight. But I had two problems. One, I didn't know that much about foot-

ball, and two, I didn't have any players. But my brother Jim had a team. He had organized a semi-pro team out in Johnstown. And Jim owed me $5,000—which was a pretty hefty sum of money in those days. So instead of paying me back, he gave me his football team. So now I had an NFL franchise.

Four years later, 1937. The middle of the Depression. The team is proving to be a costly undertaking. Here's where the racetrack comes in. We went up to Empire City—me and Buck Crouse. Buck was a pretty good middleweight. Unfortunately, he left a few of his marbles in the ring. Later he went around telling people he was Saint Francis of Assisi . . . on the level.

Joe Madden who owned a saloon in Manhattan also joined us. His brother was Owney Madden—Owney the Killer as the New York City police came to call him. I knew a number of football players were nicknamed "Killer." But this guy was the real thing. He told me once that he killed five people by the time he was 23. Favorite thing was a lead pipe wrapped in a newspaper. "Ain't nothin' scarier in New York than seein' me carrying a newspaper. Everybody knows I can't read." Whaddya say when you're sittin' in a bar havin' a drink and someone tells ya that?

Anyway, back to the racetrack story. We took our winnings from Empire City and set out for Saratoga in Joe's $150 car. Had to get out twice to push it over hills. Well, it was one winner after another, five long shots. I came close to sweeping the card. It was like that all weekend and for most of the next week. There was a writer from the *New York Herald* along with us. One day in there I lost a little, but the next day I picked up the paper and it said something like, "Rooney's Ride Continues!" So I said to that young fella, "Hey, you know I lost yesterday. What are you writing that I won for?" He said, "Mr. Rooney, if I write that you lost, I'll be back in New York working the desk. You're gonna be hot as long as I can keep you that way." And hot I stayed.

Three hundred and eighty thousand dollars.

THE CHIEF

We put all the cash in these big canvas bags and got on the train. I was scared the whole way home. I remember the look on my mother's face when we brought those bags of money into the parlor. This was 1937! She always said that money was attracted to me. I told Kass we'd never have to worry about money again. I probably would not have been able to hold on to the football team without that money. I never borrowed a dime in my life. For the longest time I didn't even know you could go to the bank and borrow money. But I got lucky. Or I was blessed.

There was no question that a lot of this money would make its way to some needy cases. I sent some of the winnings to China so Father Silas could put a new roof on his orphanage. You know who Father Silas was, don't you. It was my brother Dan. The fighter became a priest. Something happened to him along the way. He made an abrupt turn. It was when we were playing for Wheeling, livin' the life of minor-league baseball players. The late-night carousing, getting thrown out of town for starting brawls. He'd had enough.

After seminary he served in China in the '30s. He protected his parish from the marauding bandits with a baseball bat—there's that early training coming in handy again. When the Japanese Army invaded, they chased him out of China for good. He sent home the most beautiful chest. I still have it up at the house.

(Phone rings. It's Kass urging him to hurry along.)

Hello. Yes, sweetheart. 8:15 right? I've got it. Yes, I'm not finished going through the obituaries yet.

(Looking at his watch.)

All right. All right. Hey, did you tell Ice Pick about that backdoor? Okay. I know I have to stop over at West's tomorrow evening and . . . somewhere else too. I forget which funeral home. Here, maybe I have it circled.

(Picks up obit page from newspaper where several notices are circled in red.)

Yes, yes, we're still having Sunday dinner. Is everyone coming? Here it is. Freyvogel. I've got a couple over there. Yah, we're going to Schellhaas

Arthur J. Rooney and his brother Dan, playing
minor-league baseball for the Wheeling Stogies, circa 1921.
Courtesy of the Rooney family.

Monday. Yes. I've got my Mass cards. Hey! Ed Zabel's wife passed away? Yah, here it is. Clara Zabel—67. My God.

(*Circling it in the newspaper.*)

I'll call Bobby Ludwig and send a big bunch. Okay. Bye.

(*Hangs up.*)

I think it says something when it's Saturday night, and I'd rather go to a wake than receive an award.

I love wakes. I can go to three, four a night. No tux necessary. Iggy Borkowski drives me. We pull up, I get out, walk in, talk to the family. They're struck dumb usually. The widow will come up to me and say, "Mr. Rooney as I live and breathe. You know my dear husband always said he knew you and I always thought he was pulling me leg!" I got that wake habit from my days in politics. Davey Lawrence said, "Visit the sick and bury the dead. The sick and the dead might not vote, but their relatives do."

Tom Atkins as Arthur J. Rooney.
Courtesy of Suellen Fitzsimmons.

Kass goes along sometimes but not often. I've been married for almost 50 years to the most wonderful woman our God in Heaven ever created. Many of you know Kass. You know about her quick wit—she needs it to put up with my shenanigans. Father Silas once said to her it's not against God's law to go through your husband's pockets at night and extract any cash you can. And with your husband's habits, you might need it for a rainy day.

We've had a great life. We were fortunate to have a whole brood of wonderful children. She was the one did such a good job raisin' 'em. We have lived our lives all the time caring about each other . . . even more than we realized or could put into words. Then all of a sudden one morning you're looking across the breakfast table at an old woman, and you recognize that it is your wife . . . and that she is more beautiful, more radiant, more wise than ever . . . and that you don't have much time left together, but that it is really okay for the very fact that you still do have each other. That's my Kathleen.

But if I don't get out of here soon, "my Kathleen" will have my hide. She's actually looking forward to this thing tonight. She enjoys hearing all the good things about me. She believes it, too.

So before she calls again, where were we? Oh, so now I had a football team. We weren't always called the Steelers, you know. First we were the Hope Harvies. Then we were the Majestic Radios. Then the J. P. Rooneys. When we began life in the NFL, we were the Pittsburgh Pirates. We had 18 guys. Lot of former Pitt, Duquesne, and Carnegie Tech players. I paid them about a $125 a game. We played at Forbes Field. College football was still all the rage in those days, though. We only drew three, maybe 5,000 fans at a game.

Our first office was in the Fort Pitt Hotel on Liberty Avenue. "Our" meaning me and Fran Fogarty. He was the business manager. Two desks and a lot of cigar smoke. This desk right here as a matter of fact. I've had it since 1930. Lotta scuff marks. A couple drawers don't open. No worse than me. Later we got a filin' cabinet. Had a poker table in there—play til dawn sometimes.

THE CHIEF

Arthur J. Rooney and his wife, Kathleen, circa 1931.
Courtesy of the Rooney family.

Our office was on the first floor, way at the back, right next to the men's room. A lot of guys came in pullin' their flies down. We'd point them toward the next door and that was okay, but some of them would recognize me and want to strike up a conversation. Unzipped.

Since it was at the back of the building near the parking lot, many of our visitors just climbed in and out of the window instead of walkin' through the lobby. I think the management actually appreciated that. Pie Traynor — Pirate Hall of Famer — was one of those frequent visitors. After we moved over to the Union Trust Building, we were on the *fifth* floor. Pie stopped comin' in. I saw him on the corner one day and asked him where you been, and he said, "Art, I'm afraid I might forget and step out the window up there."

Meeting the payroll in the Depression was never easy. There was no television. No merchandising. Ticket sales was it. The fact that we turned a profit only once in the first 25 years is misleading. Success was just surviving. I'm not alibiing here. Other franchises were surviving *and* winning. The other club owners might have understood the game better than I did. But I had a whole lot of other business concerns to deal with. Boxing and the ponies was what was in my blood. And baseball. I would have liked to have bought the Pirates actually. But given my association with so many so-called "unsavory" characters, baseball was not interested in me. Gambling comes up again and again. It's a fact of life in pro football. We know—owners and players—that it's a delicate issue. The owners wish I wasn't in the news so much for my horseplayin' successes. I tell them to hold their pants on. I keep the two enterprises separate. I'm not about to give up the track business.

But football was fun and took care of itself. I always let the head coach run the operation. Maybe it was a mistake to hire head coaches based on whether they liked to loaf with me. Most teams the coach worried about where the players were at night. On our team the players had to worry about the coach.

Don't forget, we were the team that traded the

rights to Sid Luckman. Cut Jack Kemp and Lenny Dawson. Traded Bill Dudley—the best all-around player I've ever seen. And passed in the draft on Jim Brown. I was worried that if we were around at the millennium, we would probably cut the Second Coming.

Come to think of it, we did. His name was Johnny Unitas. Played for St. Justin's High School up on Mt. Washington. He only weighed about 130 pounds. He went to the University of Louisville where he was a star. We drafted him because he was a local boy. Well, Kies—Walt Kiesling, our head coach at that time—got it into his head that Unitas was dumb, "and he's got that stoop," Kies said. Unitas was indeed quiet, and gangly, and a little thin, but not dumb. But Kies cut him. Johnny U. then played a season here in town with the Bloomfield Rams for $6 a game. Then the Colts picked him up and the rest is history. Before he left for Baltimore, I was riding down Liberty Avenue with my son Dan and Kies and we saw Johnny walking, slouching, down the street. We pull down the window and said hello and before we drove away I told him that I hoped he would become the greatest quarterback in football. He thanked me . . . and he did of course. Maybe of all time. But as we drove off Kies just shook his head. "Dumb. Never make it."

So what was I gonna do? I had this team that lost most of its games. We played in a city where baseball was number one and college football a close second. I didn't have the time to pay that much attention. But I believed that pro football would have a future some day.

Most important, I was having fun with it, and I thought my boys would show some interest in the business. So I hung in there with it.

(Picks up tattered little notebook off the desk held together with rubber bands.)

I ran the club out of this little book. Everything about the team was right here. Lotta scuff marks here, too. Kept it in my jacket pocket. Needless to say, at that time we were not hailed as the model football operation.

The 1937 Pittsburgh Steelers, with Arthur J. Rooney, front row,

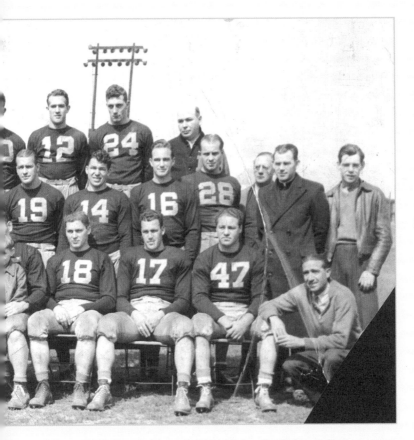

center, and his sons Dan (right) and Art Jr. (left), on laps.
Courtesy of the Pittsburgh Steelers.

In 1938 I signed Whizzer White out of Colorado University. Paid him $15,800. That was easily the highest salary pro football was paying. The other owners gave me a lot of heat. George Marshall called me from Washington and said, "What are you trying to do?" Marshall was the guy who wouldn't have any blacks on his team. "Washington is the team of the South," he would say. "Strictly a business decision." I told him a guy like Whizzer White would bring a lot of class to the league—which obviously needs it. Byron "Whizzer" White as you know went on to become a Supreme Court justice.

I just hope he's there for me if I need him.

Our fans had some things they particularly liked about us. We had a few great players and we had a lot of characters. Lot of hard drinkers—as Jimmy Finks once said, "you'd stick your head in the huddle and the smell of booze would hang there until hell froze over." Drinking was a pretty big problem and it continued all the way up until Chuck put an end to it. But we hit and we hurt the other teams. Blue-collar style. Pittsburgh style.

THE CHIEF

(Holds up or points to some players and team pictures.)

Johnny Blood, the "schizophrenic poet"—on Saturdays he played for Notre Dame as John McNally and Sundays he was Johnny Blood the NFL star. Hall of Famer John Henry Johnson. I used to love to watch him run. Tom "the Bomb" Tracy. Big Daddy Lipscomb. I could fill a book with stories about Big Daddy. Not for mixed company, though. Ernie Stautner—there was a dems and dose guy if there ever was one! Coach Buddy Parker . . . he had a tendency to drink and brood, and trade players and draft picks the night after a loss. Once, when he coached Detroit he put the whole team on waivers after a particularly bad loss. Once he cut several players over the PA system at the Detroit airport.

And of course, my poker buddy, Bobby Layne. Tough. Competitive. We got him at the tail end of his career. Singlehandedly he tried to instill our team with drive and spirit. It turned out to be too big of a job for him. Bobby would often carouse on a Saturday night before a game. Get in at

THE CHIEF

dawn. "I sleep fast," was the way he once put it.
He would then play brilliantly that day. His favorite hangout was Dante's, out there on
Brownsville Road off 51. He was always smash-
ing up his car, though. He had a particularly hard
time with Pittsburgh's streetcars. He would draw
up plays in the dirt in the middle of the huddle.
Now there's another practice that we've gotten
away from. He was the only quarterback we ever
had that never got booed. Well, almost never.
This is Pittsburgh after all.

(Holds up another picture and points to the caption.)

"The Chief and son Dan Rooney." That's me.
"The Chief." No one ever calls me that to my
face.

I don't know why that is. Do they think I don't
know? Are they afraid of what I'd say or do? The
twins gave me that name because they thought I
looked like the editor-in-chief on the *Superman*
TV show. I don't really see it, but everyone else
sure does.

Ya know — that really bothers me. Not that that is

The Chief and his son Dan Rooney, circa 1969.
Courtesy of the Pittsburgh Steelers.

my nickname, but that everyone is afraid to say it
in my presence—especially my sons.

I was tough on those boys. I'm not sure why I
was so tough. I insisted that they be regular guys
and not carry on like big shots. I boxed their ears
a few times when they got outta line. I learned

THE CHIEF

that from *my* father. I prepared them for the world. But I told my boys never let them mistake your kindness for weakness. That's the North Side version of the Golden Rule.

I insisted they go to Mass. I taught them that you receive respect when you give it. I was easygoing with everyone in the community, but I was strict with my boys. Luckily, all those times I was away at the track, on business—which was almost always—Kathleen was taking care of the boys. She helped them work out their problems, went to their football games, and she kept them from getting lost in all the hoopla that surrounded me. I wish I could have taken part in more of that.

(Phone rings.)

Hullo? Hello Rock! It's a good thing you called because I was thinking of skipping town. Whaddya mean you can't make it! If I gotta go, you gotta go.

(Listens and laughs.)

Fine then. You're going to miss seeing me in a

tux. No, I'm not letting anybody take my picture. Okay, thanks, Rock. No. I appreciate it. Okay. Bye.

(Hangs up.)

Rocky Bleier. I was afraid that Rocky would never walk again after being wounded in Vietnam. Shrapnel almost took his leg off.

Well . . . he did walk again. One Sunday, I guess it was 1969, we introduced him in a pregame ceremony. You can imagine what kind of reception our fans gave him. They stood and cheered and cheered and cheered. He walked—limped— across the field with a cane. I think the fans did something to him that day. He actually looked kind of spry. We won two Super Bowls together. Weightlifting, special shoes, learning how to run again, and "yoga," whatever that is. I don't believe I ever saw anybody ever work that hard— except maybe one or two of the guys down the mill.

In the middle of all this, the players went out on strike. Rocky was the union rep. I called him up

THE CHIEF

and let him know that if he believed in this strike not to worry about how it would affect us—me and him. I wanted him to do what he needed to do and that hopefully we'd get it settled and get back to playing football. I still shake my head about that strike. I wasn't used to being on the opposite side of my players. I knew how important unions were from everybody in the First Ward. But, with all that money already in the game . . . I couldn't understand why it came to a strike.

You know, I had tremendous offers to move the team. The propositions I got from other cities were fantastic. Back in the '50s I could have moved to Baltimore, or Buffalo, Atlanta, New Orleans, Cincinnati. Don't forget there wasn't always a big love affair between Pittsburgh and the Steelers. There were many in this area that thought I was a boob. A thick-headed, penny pinchin', Irish boob. Guys used to write letters to the newspaper saying I should be run out of town. They crucified me. Here, I've always held on to this one.

Rocky Bleier's pregame introduction at Pitt Stadium,
1969, after being wounded in Vietnam.
Courtesy of the Rooney family.

(Gets a newspaper clipping and reads to us.)

"Dear Sports Editor . . . the Steelers will never be winners because Art Rooney thinks losing is a lot less expensive. He will always be Pro Football's professional loser. There is only one thing you need to know about Rooney: he's dumb and he's cheap." I resent that. I am not cheap.

Sure that hurt. But all losers are dumb. All winners are sharp. You can't take what people say about you too seriously. I coulda been a hero in one of those bigger, football-starved towns . . . not to mention the money! But my life is here. I couldn't just pick up and go. If we were ever going to win, I wanted it to be here for the fans — even the ones of ya that think I'm dumb. I get a little upset when folks refer to those first 40 years as the bad years. Some of those years weren't so bad. I never liked losin'. But I could take it. We put a decent team on the field . . . sometimes. We competed . . . sometimes. Injuries always seemed to hurt us. We had some bad luck in our drafts. But we did have fun. We traveled by train and you got to know everybody. You got to tell a lot of stories. Players, coaches, sportswriters. Those sportswriters, they got the life of Riley. I'll tell ya. You loafed with everybody and remained friends for life. Flyin' to the games just isn't the same. The atmosphere was more enjoyable among the owners too. Sure, we fought a lot, but we were a lot closer to one another then. We had the feeling we were really creating something. I enjoyed being one of the pioneers.

And now do you see why I am so quick to defend those "Same Old Steelers?" You remember that? SOS? Same old Steelers. I know some of you used to refer to it as something other than Same Old Steelers. To me SOS meant a great bunch of guys who loved to play a sport.

But then came television. This thing here, of course, this box, is what makes our league what it is today. We were doin' all right, but the money was nothin'. Then we had a meeting with NBC. I remember it clearly. In the room were me, my son Dan, who was our real business guy, you know, and Carroll Rosenbloom, who owned the Baltimore Colts. NBC wanted to include us in the new

TV deal. He has 900,000 for the two teams, Baltimore and Pittsburgh. Rosenbloom looks at me and says, "Well Art, I have to get six. That's what I need. I can't do it unless I get $600,000." Dan gets right up out of his chair. "No way," he says, like he's going to the door. "It's split 50-50, or we're out." I said, "Wait. We can do that." Dan was mad. I didn't like it either. We went ahead with it. I figured it was 300,000 we weren't going to have otherwise.

When that contract was up, the league wanted to go with NBC again. I said that I would like the other networks to have a chance to bid. I got cursed for obstructing things. One of the owners — I won't mention his name — who was really afraid we were going to blow it, suggested that I wasn't being a very good Catholic in my negotiations. My blood started to boil. I told him in no uncertain terms you keep my religion out of it. I saw Dan out of the corner of my eye — I'm sure he thought he was gonna have to save that guy from gettin' flattened. But there was no need for that. He got the message. When the bids came in no one was cursing me anymore. We got, I don't know what we got—millions for each team. Every team. We were set. And I was miserable. Well, not miserable. But not happy. Dan said to me, "What's the matter with you? We're set here." I said, "You mark my words. You will regret this day. Television will start calling the plays. And with this kind of money around, everybody will want in on the act. Anybody with an idea or screwball scheme will come crawling out of the woodwork. Now take a look around. We do what the television executives say we do. Agents and lawyers, special trainers, weightlifting gurus, psychologists, film guys, nutritionists, scouting coordinators, draft experts. We got more assistant coaches than we had players when I started. And we're losing something in the process, and someday it will all be gone."

But I'm getting ahead of myself.

Sorry, I didn't mean to get into all of that. As I started to tell you, back in the '50s we weren't doing so hot. League officials were pressuring us

Arthur J. Rooney with sons Dan (left) and Art Jr. (right), circa 1972.
Courtesy of the Pittsburgh Steelers.

to find a new stadium. Forbes Field had 35,000
seats . . . 25,000 of 'em were bad. In '55 the city
was talking about building a new stadium. Davey
Lawrence was a big proponent. There were lots
of opponents. I'm sure you can understand why.
Taxpayers' money and all that. But my friend
Davey, he didn't tolerate interference. He wanted
a better city, and he got it. I only wish he would
have lived to see the day Three Rivers opened.

In the meantime, we moved some of our games
up Cardiac Hill into Pitt Stadium. Midway

through the 1968 season we were 0-6 and so were the Philadelphia Eagles, and we met in what was called the "O. J. Bowl." O. J. Simpson was a senior at Southern Cal and would become the number one draft choice of the team with the worst record that year. And wouldn't you know we won that game 6-3 on a field goal by Booth Lustig. But it still turned out to be the biggest off-season in the team's history.

In 1969 Dan hired Chuck Noll, our new head coach. We wanted someone who didn't act like a big shot, who would fit in Pittsburgh . . . someone who wasn't heavy into booze. We offered the job to Joe Paterno. He said no. Chuck was an assistant at Baltimore. We talked to him the day after the Colts lost to the Jets in the Super Bowl. Joe Namath, remember? Chuck's very first pick in the draft that year for us was Joe Greene from a little school in Texas. We also picked up Jon Kolb and L. C. Greenwood in that draft. We had bucked the 30-year Steeler tradition of blowing the draft. We won the first game that year, then we lost 13 in a row. Chuck kept his poise. Not only that, he kept his team. That's when I knew we had a coach—we lost 13 games in a row and the players believed in him more than ever. Chuck's an excellent teacher. He insists that his players do the little things right. He can be cool at times. Almost cold. But Chuck didn't come here to be somebody's friend. He was all business, and most important, he had a plan.

The next year we drafted Terry Bradshaw and Mel Blount and won five games. In '71 we won six games. Success comes slowly. We added Jack Ham, Dwight White, Ernie Holmes, and Mike Wagner. And that wasn't even our best draft! Chuck's plan was working. Draft good athletes and good team players. Smart guys. Noll always says, "You don't win with dummies."

Then we picked up Franco Harris. He rushed for 1,000 yards. Won Rookie of the Year. He put us over the top. We went 11–3 and got ready to face the Oakland Raiders in the playoffs.

Gloomy and damp, typical late-December Pittsburgh kind of day. One of the newspaper guys

THE CHIEF

Coach Chuck Noll, 1971.
Courtesy of the Pittsburgh Steelers.

called it a ghostly gray sky. Little bit of the Irish poet in that writer.

I was watchin' from upstairs, and the thing I remember most about it was the tension in that stadium. We'd never played in that kind of atmosphere. Three hours almost, and no one had scored a touchdown. We were ahead 6-0 on two field goals, but it just didn't *feel* like we were ahead. How can you be ahead for nearly 59 minutes of a football game and never *feel* like you're ahead? I don't know. I guess when you're a Steeler fan, you know what I mean. It just never felt right, that day, that game. It was great to see the boys in a big playoff game finally, because they'd worked so hard, and they were good guys. I was real proud of 'em.

At the two-minute warning, Oakland was driving on us. They had a quarterback, Kenny Stabler. The Snake. He ran about 30 yards down the sideline for a touchdown. I can't say that I didn't expect something like that, but I was heartsick sitting there watching the Raiders kick the extra point and go ahead 7–6. "That's it," I thought.

There was 1:13 to go, and I got up and went to the elevator because I wanted to be in the locker room when the fellas came in. Tell them how good I thought they played and how proud I was of them. To be the first to wish them a Happy New Year and to enjoy their off-season, about how I was looking forward to seeing them next July because we had a fine team with a great future. I was thinking something like that when the elevator doors opened on the ground floor.

I'll tell ya, the noise hit me like a tornado. I thought it *was* a tornado. I thought the stadium was falling down. I walked down the tunnel toward the field, and people were running and screaming with great big smiles. Yelling and hooting. That's when it hit me. Jesus. Mary. And Joseph. We won this game! WE WON THIS GAME!

It's been called ever since . . . the Immaculate Reception. Here's what the play looked like. 66 Circle Option.

Terry Bradshaw! Scrambling! Twenty-two seconds left! To Frenchy Fuqua and *Bang!* with Jack Tatum. And gosh Franco Harris . . . IT'S CAUGHT OUTTA THE AIR! . . . and I never saw a second of it.

I was too busy feeling bad for them that I never thought to feel good enough about them to think they could pull it out. Maybe I thought that because that's the way it had always been, the way it was supposed to be.

And that changed a lot, you know? What Franco did for us on that day.

Chuck said that a lot of guys started really believing in themselves after that. And our fans started really believing. After Franco's catch, that SOS stuff went away. So did 40 years of losing. I love Franco Harris.

I sometimes think about what if Franco doesn't make that play? What if Jack Tatum, instead of trying to take Frenchy's head off, just tackles him and the clock runs out? What if the ball doesn't make it all the way back to Franco?

Then what?

Do we go 4-10 the next year? Do we go back to being the Same Old Steelers? Does Chuck get fired? Am I back to being a boob? Do our fans have even more bad luck heaped on them?

But Tatum didn't play it smart. And Franco did catch it before it touched the carpet.

Miami beat us the next week. That was tough. But we had confidence going into the next season. And guess what? We went 10-4 and Oakland beat us in the playoffs. And so it goes. That's the thing about the NFL—there's 20-some other teams lookin' to do the same thing you are.

But finally, the year before last, we draft Lynn Swan, Jack Lambert, John Stallworth, and Mike Webster. Anybody ever have a draft better than that? I don't think so. Anybody ever play any better than we did that fall? I don't think so. Now we have the whole rest of the league wondering if anyone's ever been better than these Steelers. You know what? I don't think so. And suddenly—I mean, you know, suddenly some 42 years after the J. P. Rooneys got into the NFL— we won the Super Bowl.

One minute I was congratulating our players, the next I'm on national TV. Rozelle is talking to me, and I can't quite understand what he was saying. Where are my sons? Where is Chuck? Where are my sons?

(He gets the ball, and looks it over as though transported.)

No wonder this felt so heavy.

I just never imagined myself in that position and then when I got there . . . I sure didn't have anything prepared to say. For a guy that was always so good at moving on to the next thing, suddenly I had no place to go.

And there was Andy Russell coming at me with this in his hand. Andy who'd been with us through many a bad time. And I thought. "No, this isn't for me. This is for the fans."

I read a column the other day that said there are

two kinds of fans in Pittsburgh right now. Fans that have lost their jobs and fans that are going to. When things were going good for them, when the mills were humming and the sky was black, their outlook was bright. They had steady jobs and they could spend a few bucks on a couple a pitchers of Iron City, or go to Kennywood on Slovak Day or Italian Day. They could see their Steelers lose on Sunday. Now that the sky over Pittsburgh is clear and their outlook is black, we are their champions.

When Lambert takes his teeth out on Sunday and slams into somebody like a locomotive, the fans are the steam in that engine. It's *their* passion. That's why they love us so much. We remind them that winning is always possible.

A life can go like the Immaculate Reception. Mine sure did. Some long, improbable passes. Some major collisions. There always seemed to be a Jack Tatum waiting for you downfield.

But you never play the game alone. I played it with Billy Conn. My brother Dan. Senator

Coyne. Bobby Layne. Stella Guier. Squawker Mullen. Chris McCormick. The Irish First Ward. I played it with the whole city of Pittsburgh.

Sometimes the ball hits the carpet . . . with a weak splash. Most times there isn't a Franco to catch it. You just have to pick yourself up and move on to the next thing. But sometimes you do catch it. You gotta be ready for that one too.

(Pauses, has a sudden thought.)

Do you want to see it? I have it right here.

(He threads the projector, gets the lights and turns the projector on. We all watch it one more time together. When he brings the lights back up, he is dressed in his tux.)

I never get tired of watching that.

(The phone rings.)

Hello. Yes, okay. I'm getting my coat on. I'll be there in five minutes, and then we'll go. And Kass . . . you know what, let's just walk around and go in the front door tonight. Good-bye.

Jack Tatum's ferocious hit on Frenchy Fuqua sends the ball
back toward Franco Harris, seconds prior to the Immaculate
Reception, December 23, 1972.
Courtesy of the Pittsburgh Steelers.

*(Hangs up. Places cigars in pocket. Turns off lights.
He remembers the speech and retrieves it. He glances
once more at the office, and closes the door. Lights
fade.)*

(End of play.)

THE CHIEF

Arthur J. Rooney with four Super Bowl trophies.
Courtesy of the Pittsburgh Steelers.

Acknowledgments

The authors would like to express their appreciation to the following individuals:

Arthur Rooney Jr., Dan Rooney, Jim Rooney, Mike Fabus, Roy McHugh, Ed Kiely, Myron Cope, Geraldine Glenn, Bob McCartney, Monica Bowin, Michael Essad, Mark Desch, Joe Hartnett, Celeste Parrendo, Gay Kahkonen, Kelly Yann, Justin Pelissero, Todd Kulik, Nikole Lopretto, and Kari Kramer.

About the Playwrights

Rob Zellers has been the education director at Pittsburgh Public Theater for 20 years. Over this time he has created numerous programs and worked with thousands of students in acting, technical theater, and playwriting. His new play, *Harry's Friendly Service*, will be produced at Pittsburgh Public Theater in June 2009. His work on *The Chief* is dedicated to his wife, Jean, and his daughter, Alexa.

Gene Collier has written about sports and politics in Philadelphia and Pittsburgh for more than 30 years and has twice been nominated for the Pulitzer Prize, losing spectacularly both times. His alleged humor can be heard weekly on WDVE, and he persists in ill-advised attempts at stand-up comedy. His work on *The Chief* is dedicated to his wonderful wife, Gerry, without whose encouragement it would have been impossible, and to the inspiration of his sons, Sean and Andy.

About
Pittsburgh Public Theater

Founded in 1975, The Public is the flagship theater company of Pittsburgh's vibrant cultural scene. Led by Producing Artistic Director Ted Pappas, The Public is nationally renowned for the wide range and remarkable quality of its work, including international classics, great American plays, musicals of exceptional merit, and world premieres, such as August Wilson's *Jitney* and *King Hedley II*, Naomi Wallace's *Things of Dry Hours*, and the Lynn Ahrens/Stephen Flaherty musical *The Glorious Ones*.

Rob Zellers and Gene Collier.
Courtesy of Suellen Fitzsimmons.